A23448

Costume in Context
The Stuarts

Jennifer Ruby

B.T. Batsford Ltd, London

Foreword

When studying costume it is important to understand the difference between fashion and costume. Fashion tends to predict the future – that is, what people *will* be wearing – and very fashionable clothes are usually worn only by people wealthy enough to afford them. For example, even today, the clothes that appear in fashionable magazines are not the same as those being worn by the majority of people in the street. Costume, on the other hand, represents what people are actually wearing at a given time, which may be quite different from what is termed 'fashionable' for their day.

Each book in this series is built round a fictitious family. By following the various members, sometimes over several generations – and the people with whom they come into contact – you will be able to see the major fashion developments of the period and compare the clothing and lifestyles of people from all walks of life. You will meet servants, soldiers, street-sellers and beggars as well as the very wealthy, and you will see how their different clothing reflects their particular occupations and circumstances.

Major social changes are mentioned in each period and you will see how clothing is adapted as people's needs and attitudes change. The date list will help you to understand more fully how historical events affect the clothes that people wear.

Many of the drawings in these books have been taken from contemporary paintings. During the course of your work perhaps you could visit some museums and art galleries yourself in order to learn more about the costumes of the period you are studying from the artists who painted at that time.

Acknowledgments

I would like to acknowledge the sources for the colour plates in this book as follows: 'Fashionable couple', after Rubens; Charles I after Van Dyck; 'Fashionable lady', after G. Honthorst; 'Two serving maids' after Francis Millet and Nicholas Maes; 'Commonwealth fashions' after Dion Calthrop; 'Fashions for 1670' after Brooke; 'Rich and poor' after Jan Steen and Mignard; 'Female fashion for 1693' after I.D. St Jean.
   My grateful thanks to Mike and Angela Overton for the fascinating information they provided on the Sally Lunn Coffee House in Bath.

Typeset by Tek-Art Ltd, Kent
and printed in Great Britain by
R J Acford, Chichester, Sussex
for the publishers
B.T. Batsford Ltd
4 Fitzhardinge Street
London W1H 0AH

ISBN 0 7134 5604 3

Contents

Date List   4
Introduction   5

c. 1610
A Young Man of Fashion   8
A Lady-in-Waiting   10

c. 1631
The Nobleman in Later Life   12
The Nobleman's Wife   14

c. 1632
The Nobleman's Children   16

c. 1633
Four Servants   18

c. 1639
A Yeoman Farmer and a Farm
    Labourer   20
The Farmer's Family   22

c. 1644
A Cavalry Officer   24
A Pikeman   26
A Musketeer   27

1651
A Disguise for Prince Charles   28
A Miller   30
A Blacksmith   31
A Fashionable Lady   32

c. 1655
A Fashionable Gentleman   33

A Quaker Family   34

c. 1663
A Nobleman at Court   36
The Nobleman's Wife   38

1665
A Doctor   40
A Watchman   41

1666
A Family in the Great Fire   42

c. 1667
An Actress   44
A Highwayman   46

c. 1680
A Lady of Fashion   48
A Gentleman of Fashion   50

c. 1685
A Coffee Shop   52
Two Street-Vendors   54

c. 1693
The New Fashions   56
Eleanor's Children   58

Conclusion   60
Glossary   62
Book List   63
Places to Visit   63
Things to Do   64

lady of fashion
(c. 1680)

Date List

1603   James I comes to the throne. Fashions retain the Spanish influence of the previous century. Farthingales, padded breeches, ruffs and stiff collars are popular.

1620   Pilgrim Fathers sail to America. Merchants soon set up trading links with the new colonies.

1625   Death of James I. Succeeded by his son, Charles I. French fashions now dominate the English scene. Smooth lines, plain fabrics, falling collars and lace trimmings are prevalent. Puritan clothes are now seen more frequently, due to the growing numbers of religious dissenters. They wear plain clothes of dark cloths, and white collars and cuffs.

1642   The beginning of the English Civil War. Many families are split.

1649   Execution of Charles I. The start of the Commonwealth. Fashions become much more subdued.

1651   The battle of Worcester. Charles II fails to regain the throne and escapes to France.

1652   The first London coffee house opens. Fashionable gentlemen meet here to drink coffee and discuss the news.

1658   Death of Cromwell. He is succeeded by his son.

1660   The Restoration. Charles returns from France, bringing the French fashions with him. There is a new extravagance in clothing with frills, lace, ribbons and bows being worn in abundance by both sexes. French wigs quickly become fashionable.

1665   The Great Plague.

1666   The Great Fire. At about this time we see the very beginnings of men's suits. The doublet is becoming unfashionable and waistcoats and coats are seen more and more.

1675   Charles II orders his subjects not to wear foreign lace as a protection for the English lace industry.

1680s   There is an influx of French Huguenot refugees, who are skilled silk weavers and designers. They are absorbed into the English textile industry, which means that silk begins to be produced at home.

1685   Death of Charles II. He is succeeded by his brother James II.

1688   The 'Bloodless Revolution'. William of Orange is invited to England to claim the English throne. James escapes to France.

1690   The distinctive *fontange* headdress becomes fashionable for women, as does the bustle.

1690   A French Protestant refugee establishes the first calico printing factory near London. By 1700 calico printing is flourishing in many parts of south-east England.

1694   Queen Mary dies of smallpox.

1697   Ban introduced on French and Flemish lace.

1697   Travelling salesmen, who provide small accessories and trimmings for people living in isolated areas, are licensed in order to safeguard the public against dishonest pedlars.

1701   Ban introduced on the household use and wear of Indian cottons, as English wool and silk weavers see them as a threat.

1702   William dies and Mary's sister Anne becomes Queen.

1714   Anne dies. All of her 17 grandchildren have predeceased her, so the throne passes to George I – the first Hanoverian.

Introduction

The seventeenth century was a period of great turbulence. One monarch was executed and another was deposed; there were religious arguments, a civil war, a plague epidemic and the Great Fire of London. It was also a time of contrasts – for example, the sombre and austere rule of Cromwell and Parliament compared with the gaiety and exuberance of the court of Charles II. All these events had a great effect on the fashions of the time, which reflected the various changes in society.

The century opened with the stiff, formal costumes of James I's court. The ladies wore wheel farthingales, the men had tiny waists and padded breeches, and both sexes wore starched ruffs or high collars. These fashions had originated in Spain during the previous century and were still very popular. The clothes were made of silks, satins and brocades, many of which had been imported. Contrasting patterns were worn together, along with many jewels and ornaments.

These fashions gave way to the quieter and more elegant clothes of Charles I and his French wife, Henrietta Maria. They favoured the French styles which soon began to dominate English fashions. Clothes became smoother and more loose fitting, falling collars were favoured over ruffs, and plain materials were preferred to the extravagant patterns that had gone before.

At the same time, various religious groups, known as Puritans, began to develop. They wanted to purify the church and disapproved wholeheartedly of ostentatious fashions, considering that luxurious dress was immoral. They dressed in quiet and conservative clothes made of dark wool cloths relieved only by white collars and cuffs. Some Puritans went to America to try and create their own ideal society. Soon, astute merchants in England set up trading links with the new American colonies. This meant that England was now trading on a wider basis outside Europe. Another of these trading links was with India, from where cotton was imported.

During the Commonwealth (1649-60) a great many leisure pursuits were forbidden – for example, theatres were closed, football and wrestling were banned, and there were laws against bear- and bull-baiting. People were almost compelled to live by the 'Good Book', and it seemed as if this austerity was reflected in dress. Although it is not true to say that everyone adopted the Puritan style of clothing, nevertheless, fashions were more subdued than formerly. In any case, the wearing of frivolous accessories and fancy frills would probably indicate that you were a Royalist supporter and would invite unfavourable comments.

Puritan dress (c. 1650)

c. 1629

c. 1644

c. 1630

c. 1629

c. 1630

c. 1617

c. 1700

6

In 1660 Charles II returned from his exile in France, bringing the French fashions with him, and it was as if there was a 'letting go' after the solemnity of the previous 11 years. Theatres were re-opened, and gambling, dancing and merrymaking were prevalent – so much so that the Puritans felt that the Great Plague and Fire were a punishment for such extravagant living. Ribbons, bows, frills, flounces and lace trimmings were worn in abundance by both sexes.

French styles continued to influence English fashions throughout the rest of the Stuart period, even though William and Mary were politically opposed to France. This time saw also the beginnings of the man's suit, which, with moderations, has survived to our own century.

In the 1680s, England began to acquire its own silk industry. This was largely because many French Huguenot weavers and designers fled to England as refugees from religious persecution and brought their skills with them. They were soon absorbed into the English textile industry and this eventually led to cheaper silks as they no longer had to be imported.

Materials were very expensive throughout the century, however, and both men's and women's clothes were usually made by tailors. This meant that the fashions described above were costly and worn only by the rich. The rich included many of the rising middle classes such as doctors, lawyers and merchants. This was an age in which social position was associated with the possession of a fashionable wardrobe, so many worked hard in order to afford good clothes for themselves and their families.

For poorer people it was a different story. Their clothes changed very little during the century. They could not possibly afford to wear fashionable clothes and, besides, frills, ribbons and flounces would have been impractical when working. In addition to this, communication was a much slower process than it is today, and fashions took a long time to travel from court, where they originated, to country areas. Country folk and poorer people in the towns tended to wear simple garments made of cotton, wool, linen and leather rather than the expensive satins and silks of fashion.

In this book you will meet people from all walks of life – the wealthy and fashionable, servants, farm workers, an actress, a doctor and even a highwayman. While you are reading, think carefully about each character's background. This will help you to understand a little more about what it was like to live and work in Stuart times.

street seller
(c. 1700)

A Young Man of Fashion, c. 1610

Here is Robert, the 15-year-old son of a nobleman. He is at the court of King James I. His fashionable clothes are stiff and formal and highly decorated.

He is wearing a close-fitting, embroidered jacket called a doublet, which has a tabbed skirt and sleeves with wings. His trunk hose, or breeches, match the the doublet and are padded, emphasizing his hips. His semi-circular collar is starched and supported by a wire frame called an underpropper. This frame was usually bound with gold, silver or silk thread. The lace cuffs of his shirt are visible at his wrists, and his low-heeled shoes are decorated with ribbon rosettes. He is wearing silk stockings and carrying his leather gloves.

Robert's doublet and breeches are fastened together with points. Points were ties, rather like our laces, and they usually had metal tags, called aiglets, on the ends. Each morning, Robert's valet has to help him with his points and make sure that he is laced up correctly and that everything is neatly in place. How long do you think it would take him to get dressed? How long does it take *you* to get dressed in the mornings?

Do you think these padded breeches would be uncomfortable? James I disliked padding in any form but he used to wear a great deal of it himself because he felt that it gave him protection from would-be assassins!

Robert is clean-shaven and has short hair like other young men of his age. He is wearing a fashionable ear string. This is a few strands of black silk threaded through his left ear and left to dangle on to his shoulder.

On the opposite page you can see other items from his wardrobe.

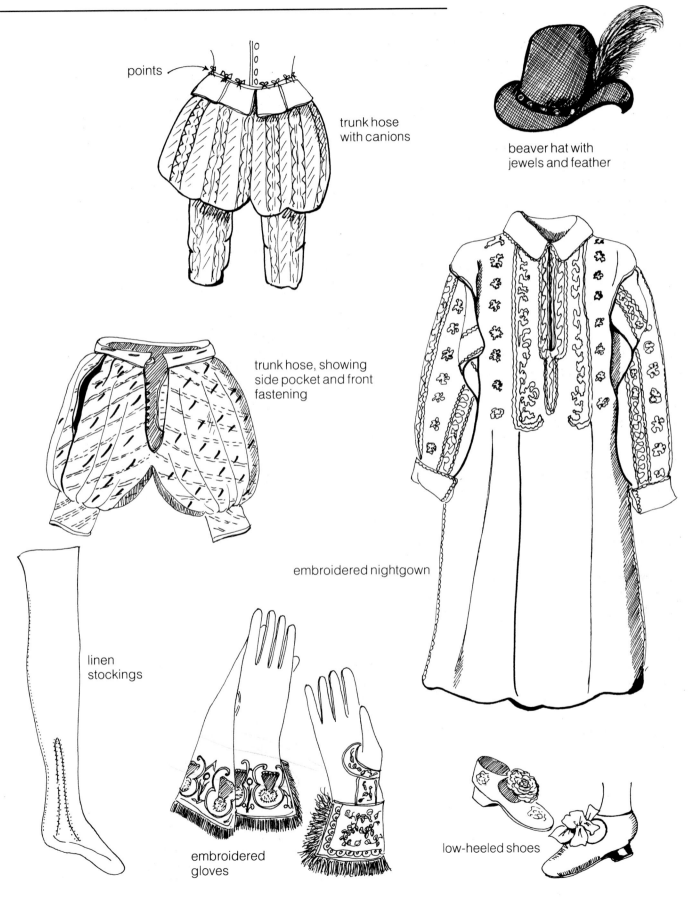

points

trunk hose
with canions

beaver hat with
jewels and feather

trunk hose, showing
side pocket and front
fastening

embroidered nightgown

linen
stockings

embroidered
gloves

low-heeled shoes

A Lady-in-Waiting, c. 1610

This is Mary, who is betrothed to Robert. She is a lady-in-waiting to the Queen. As she is at court, Mary is wearing fashionable and expensive clothes.

Her dress is made from Italian brocaded silk and has a tightly fitted, low-necked bodice, the neckline of which is filled in with cotton lawn. The sleeves are also close fitting and have hanging sham sleeves at the back. Underneath her skirt she is wearing a farthingale petticoat (pictured opposite). This was a wheel-shaped structure made of whalebone or wire and covered with silk. It was this petticoat that gave ladies the distinctive shape of the period.

Like Robert, Mary is wearing a semi-circular collar supported with wire, and on her head she has an embroidered linen cap called a cornet, or shadow. She carries a feather fan, and the ring on her left hand is secured by a ribbon at her wrist, as is the fashion.

Queen Anne admired the wheel farthingale and because of this it was regarded as highly fashionable and it increased in size. Once, at a grand masque at court, several of the ladies became wedged in the passage and blocked the entrance to the hall so that more than half the guests never managed to get in at all! After this, James I tried to ban the wheel farthingale from court but he was unsuccessful because the Queen favoured it. The other type of farthingale that was common at this time was the French roll (popularly known as the 'bum roll'), which was worn under the dress and accentuated the hips but not in such a pronounced way as the wheel did.

Other items from Mary's wardrobe are pictured here. An interesting feature of the corset is the small front pocket, in which Mary would probably place a bottle containing fresh flowers. Although ladies looked very beautiful they rarely washed, so the posy of flowers was used to counteract unpleasant odours!

How do you think it would feel to be encased in such tight-fitting garments all day? What sort of problems might be caused by wearing a wheel farthingale?

feather fan with jewelled handle

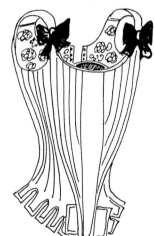

corset laced at back – front pocket to hold 'bosom bottle' containing water for fresh flowers

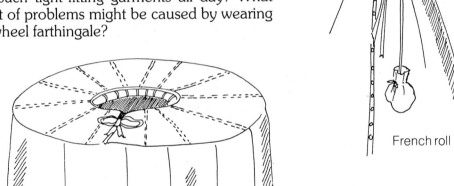

French roll

white brocade boudoir slipper

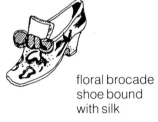

floral brocade shoe bound with silk

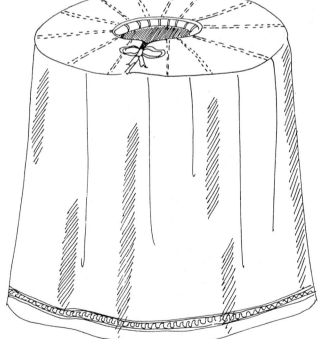

French wheel farthingale

enamelled silver perfume case

high-cut brocade shoe with lace collar

The Nobleman in Later Life, c. 1631

It is now 1631. Robert and Mary have been married for some years and are living with their children and servants on their estate in Worcestershire. Charles I has been on the throne since 1625 and sets the fashion with his taste for elegant, beautiful clothes.

You can see from Robert's outfit that the doublet is now longer, the tabs having been replaced by a deep basque (the band of material attached to the waistline). It is decorated with slashes on the front and sleeves, through which you can see the shirt underneath. His matching breeches are longer and less bulky than formerly and are tied with ribbon just below the knee.

It is now the custom for fashionable men to wear boots for walking as well as for riding, and Robert is wearing his with the tops rolled down with 'butterfly' spur leathers – so called because of their shape. He is also wearing boot hose over his silk stockings in order to protect them from the inner surface of the boots. The tops of the boot hose are visible just below the breeches.

The stiff, wired collars that you saw earlier have now largely been replaced by softer lace collars. Sometimes Robert might wear a falling ruff, as pictured on the right, which is a cross between a lace collar and the stiff ruff.

Like King Charles, Robert wears his hair longer on one side than on the other. Some men wore what was called a love-lock. This was a tress of hair grown long and usually curled or waved and brought forward from the nape of the neck to fall over the chest and then tied with a ribbon. Many men dyed their hair using nutmeg. Can you see any similarities between these hairdressing ideas and some of our styles today?

Also pictured here are a few of Robert's accessories. On the right he is wearing a 'Cavalier' hat decorated with an ostrich feather. Pantoffles, or overshoes, were very popular at this time, as wealthy men and women wished to protect their fine boots and shoes when out walking in the filthy streets.

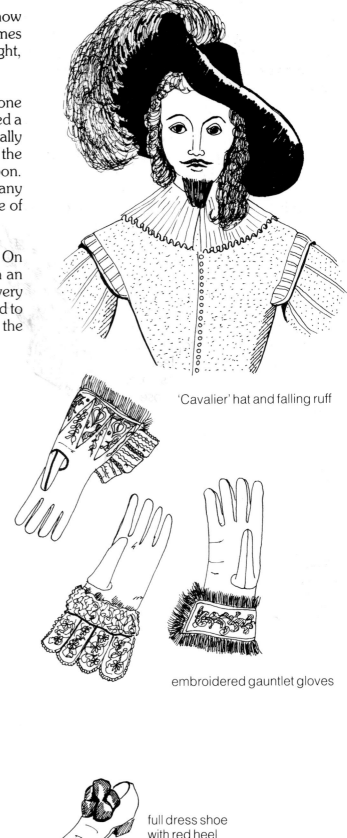

'Cavalier' hat and falling ruff

ruffles at the
end of breeches,
lace-topped
boot hose,
leather boot
and overshoe

embroidered gauntlet gloves

buff leather
boot with triple
lace frill

shoe with
side opening
and pantoffle

full dress shoe
with red heel
and rose decoration

The Nobleman's Wife, c. 1631

You can see from Mary's costume that fashions for women have become much softer and more elegant than previously. Plain materials are seen more frequently than patterned ones, and the farthingale has disappeared, giving a smoother, softer line to the female figure.

As usual, these fashions were being set by the court. Charles I's Queen, Henrietta Maria, who was French, was not extravagant in her clothes (unlike the two queens before her), and it was from her that fashionable ladies took their lead.

Mary is wearing a satin dress with a low neckline which is filled with a fine lawn partlet. The bodice and skirt are separate, as with most dresses at this time. The bodice is tabbed, and the sleeves have been paned (cut into strips). The panes are secured with ribbon bows. Mary has lace cuffs and white gloves. The wired lace collar of the dress is edged with lace which combines with the lace collar over the bodice.

She wears her hair with the back drawn into a bun, the side pieces curled and a short fringe. The style is decorated with pearls.

Mary often goes without a hat but she always takes great care to protect her complexion. In the summer she wears a veil over her face, as freckles and a suntan are considered harmful and disfiguring. In the winter she might wear a velvet or silk mask for protection. In fact, it was considered immodest for a lady to go out at night without a mask (this was the origin of the saying 'bare-faced' meaning 'too bold').

Paint, powder, patches and perfume were all fashionable at this time, and the use of rouge was common. In the picture on the left Mary is wearing a face patch. This is made of silk and is kept in place with mastic, a gum taken from the bark of certain trees.

Perhaps you could find out more about seventeenth-century make-up. Try to discover what ladies put on to their faces, if they dyed their hair and, if so, what kinds of dye they used.

In the pictures on this page Mary is wearing other garments from her wardrobe. Why do you think it would be necessary for her to wear a furred cape when *indoors*?

See if you can find a picture of Queen Henrietta Maria. Compare her clothes with those of Queen Anne (James I's Queen). What are the differences in style? Which style do you think would be more comfortable?

lace neckerchief – fan suspended from ribbon belt

veil over face for protection

rear view of hairstyle – furred cape for indoor wear

The Nobleman's Children, c. 1632

Here are Lord Robert's four children. Cecily, the eldest, is nine years old and is dressed as a smaller version of her mother. She is wearing a satin dress with a basque bodice, paned sleeves and a lace collar. She has a feather and pearls decorating her hair and a fan suspended from her belt. She is lifting up a corner of her dress, revealing her underskirt beneath and her pretty shoe roses. Underneath her clothes she is wearing a corset like her mother's.

It was the custom at this time to dress little boys almost indentically to girls until they were six or seven years old. Only then were they 'breeched' and put into their first suits. Henry is four years old and is wearing an embroidered nightgown with slashed sleeves and a falling collar. He has a handkerchief, known as a muckinder, suspended from his waist and an embroidered coif on his head.

James is two years old. He is wearing a satin doublet and matching petticoat with lace trimmings and a lace coif.

Small babies were bound tightly in strips of cloth, known as swaddling bands, as it was thought that they might harm themselves if they were able to move their limbs around. Baby Honor is lying cocooned in her swaddling bands and beautifully embroidered covers. Do you think it would be harmful to restrict a baby's movements in this way? You can see more baby clothes in the pictures below. They are made of linen and have been embroidered with a linen cord.

In Stuart times many children died before reaching maturity. You could investigate some of the reasons for this and compare seventeenth-century attitudes towards child care with those of today.

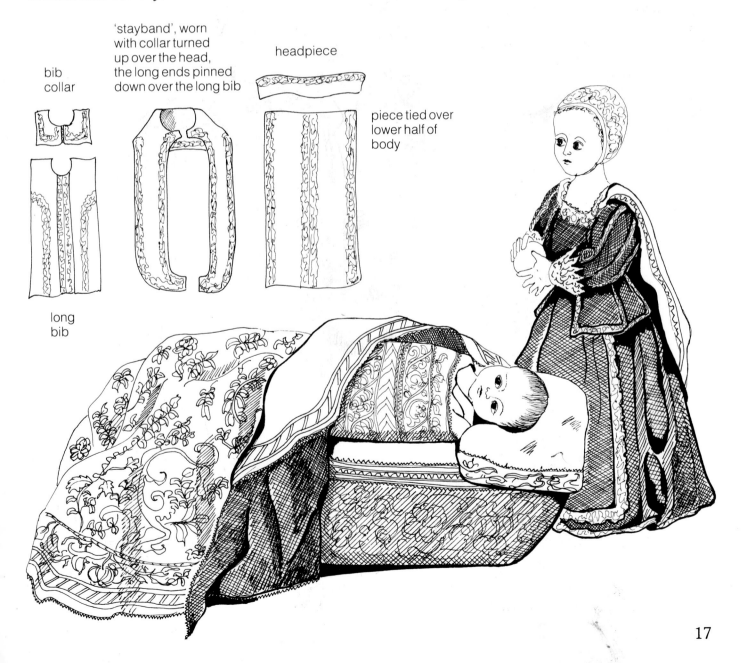

bib collar

'stayband', worn with collar turned up over the head, the long ends pinned down over the long bib

headpiece

piece tied over lower half of body

long bib

Four Servants, c. 1633

In Stuart times the costumes worn by servants varied according to their position. For example, the upper ranks of household servants, such as valets and ladies' maids, tended to come from fairly affluent families and, therefore, dressed in the fashion of the day (although not quite as ostentatiously as their employers). The lower ranks, however, dressed more plainly.

Lord Robert has many servants on his estate and some of them are pictured here.

On the far left you can *see* Ruth, who is a housemaid. She is dressed quite fashionably as she tends to work in the main house and is expected to be smart and neat at all times. The bodice of her dress has slashes in the sleeves and front, through which you can see her chemise. She is wearing a falling ruff and has lace cuffs and an embroidered lace cap. Her apron is pinned to her belt to reveal the embroidery on her skirt. In contrast, Matty, the kitchen maid, is very plainly dressed. She is wearing a coarse linen dress and apron and a white linen neckerchief and hood. All her hair is covered and she has none of Ruth's fashionable curls.

Ralph is a page boy. Lord Robert likes to show off his wealth by having his pages splendidly dressed, so he provides Ralph with fashionable clothes like those pictured here. Ralph is wearing a doublet, trimmed around the waist with ribbon bows, a falling ruff and cloak bag breeches which are oval in shape and end at the knee. He has garters and large shoe roses and is carrying his cloak and beaver hat.

John, the little boy employed to turn the spit in the kitchen, is not very happy. He is tired and has just been reprimanded by the cook. He is wearing only his shirt and ragged breeches. See if you can find out more about how each of these boys would have spent his days. From what kind of backgrounds do you think they would have come?

A Yeoman Farmer and a Farm Labourer, c. 1639

In Stuart society, a 'yeoman' was someone whose status was higher than that of a 'husbandman' but below that of a 'gentleman'. A typical yeoman would own a few hundred acres of land and have his own farmhouse or be a tenant farmer with a long security of tenure. He would work hard and put back the profits he obtained from his crops, sheep or cattle into his farms and stock. He would probably be quite well educated and have a reputation for being careful rather than extravagant.

Robin, pictured here, is a yeoman farmer. His dress is of good quality and is reasonably fashionable but is not, of course, as flamboyant as the nobleman's. He is wearing a linen doublet and breeches, leather boots with cuffs and butterfly spur leathers, and a cloak. He is carrying his beaver hat.

Robin has been talking to Richard, one of the farm labourers. Richard's clothes are simple and practical, consisting of a shirt, a long jacket made of coarse linen, baggy breeches, woollen hose and leather button boots. He carries a leather pouch on his belt.

Although farm workers tended to wear old-fashioned clothes like these, the fashionable 'sugarloaf' hat that Richard is wearing here was very popular. It had a high crown and broad brim and was often made of felt. It was probably very comfortable for working in.

For hot weather and heavy work Richard and the other labourers wear only their shirts and breeches.

Perhaps you could do a project on farm life in the seventeenth century and find out more about the yeoman farmers and how they used to live.

The Farmer's Family, c. 1639

Here is Robin's wife, Hannah, with three of their children.

Alice, who is ten years old, is looking after William. She is wearing a plain linen dress with long sleeves and a white cotton hood, neckerchief and apron. Her little brother is only three so he is still in his 'petticoats' (which means that he has not yet been 'breeched'). He is wearing a bibbed apron and a linen gown.

Alice helps her mother a great deal and together they make butter, cheese, jam and preserves. They also do spinning, weaving and knitting. Here, Alice is busy knitting a woollen hat for William.

Hannah is in the courtyard of their farmhouse with five-year-old Elizabeth. She is wearing a white, lace-edged hood which has been pinned up at the back, a neckerchief and a light-coloured linen gown. The skirt of her gown is tucked into her belt to keep it clean while she is doing her housework. Over her shoes she is wearing wooden pattens to protect her shoes from the mud and dirt outside the house. These are raised off the ground by an iron ring and fastened to her feet with leather straps.

Little Elizabeth is wearing a coif, a linen gown and a white, bibbed apron.

Compare these clothes with those worn by the nobleman and his family. Look at the children's dress in particular. Which children do you think are the most comfortable?

A Cavalry Officer, c. 1644

It is now 1644 and the country is in the grip of civil war. The fight is between the King and Parliament and many men, both young and old, have become soldiers.

Those who fought for the King were called Cavaliers. Those who fought for Parliament were called Roundheads, because of their short hairstyles.

In 1642, when the war began, people had to choose which side to support. For some it was an easy decision, but for others it was a sad and difficult one. There was often great heartache when men fought against their friends and fellow countrymen. Sometimes, even families split, with brothers joining opposing sides.

For many people there was no choice to be made – they simply followed their master. Here is Ralph, the page boy you met earlier. He has joined the war with Lord Robert on the King's side and is now a cavalry officer. Lord Robert's son Henry is not yet 16, but when he is he will join his father and Ralph in the fighting.

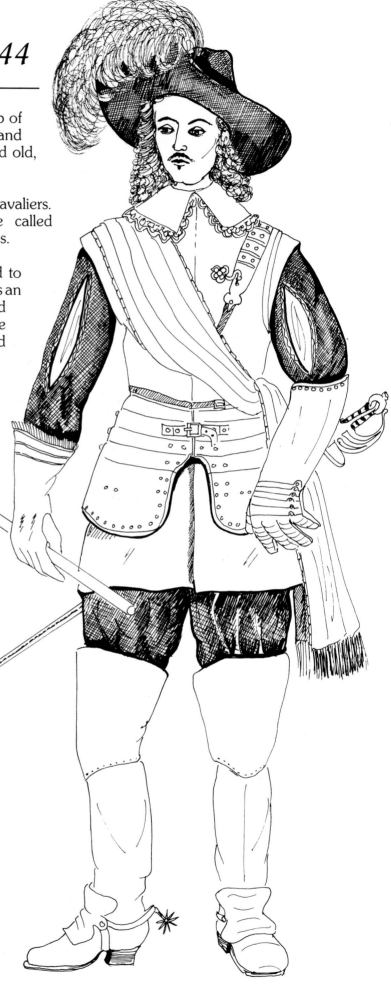

When the fighting began many men found that a full suit of armour was too heavy and too hot. Consequently, they began to wear the minimum amount of armour over a buff coat, or simply a buff coat on its own. Buff was ox-hide treated with oil, and the coats were fitted and sometimes sleeveless, so that the doublet sleeves were visible.

In the picture on the left, Ralph is wearing some armour over his clothes. He has on a breast and back plate, a skirt, and a gauntlet on his left arm. Underneath his armour he has on a doublet, a buff coat, breeches and thigh-length leather boots. In his right hand he carries a baton. He also wears a shoulder sash and a Cavalier hat.

Because there was no uniform for either army it was often difficult to pick out the enemy in the excitement of a battle. Sometimes, soldiers were given secret signs before a battle commenced. For example, before the battle of Marston Moor the Roundheads put a piece of white paper in their hats so that they could recognize each other. When Parliamentarian Sir Thomas Fairfax found himself cut off from his own men he simply removed the piece of paper from his hat and rode through the lines of Cavalier soldiers as though he were one of them and rejoined his own side!

On this page you can see examples of soldiers' clothing. Compare these with some of the uniforms of today's soldiers. What are the main differences?

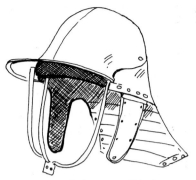

'lobster-tail' helmet, back and breast plates

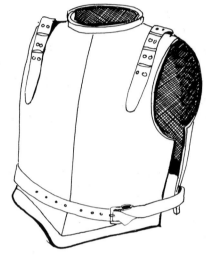

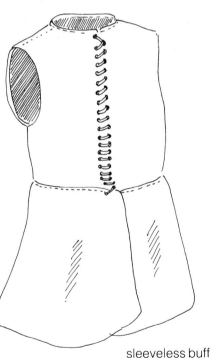

sleeveless buff coat or jerkin

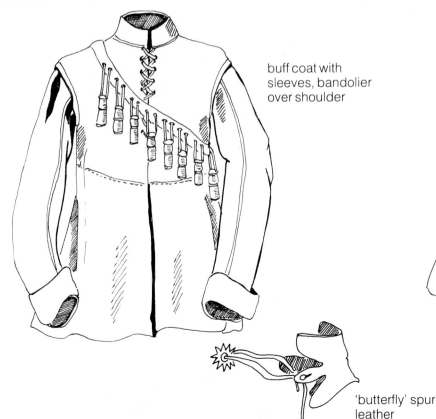

buff coat with sleeves, bandolier over shoulder

'butterfly' spur leather

A Pikeman, c. 1644

This is Edmund, the eldest son of Robin, the yeoman farmer. He is a pikeman and, like his father, is fighting for Parliament. Pikemen had to be strong, tall men because their pikes were 5 metres long and very heavy. In defence, pikemen stood with their pikes levelled out to prevent the enemy from piercing their lines. When attacking, they used their pikes to push the other side back.

Over his doublet and buff coat Edmund is wearing a helmet, breast and back plates and an armoured skirt. His breeches are tied at the knee with ribbon bows, and he has thick hose and stout leather shoes.

Can you imagine how heavy the pike would be? Try and visualize its length. How would it feel to fight with such a heavy weapon whilst wearing armour?

Although Edmund and his father are for the cause of Parliament, they do not believe that they are fighting against their King – they see themselves as trying to save the King from all his mistakes and bad advisers. Robin is very sad because he and Edmund have been unable to persuade another of his sons, Simon, to join them. Simon feels that the King has 'Divine Right' and that it is, therefore, wrong to fight against him. Simon has joined the Cavaliers as a musketeer.

the head of the pike

A Musketeer, c. 1644

Around his neck, Simon is wearing a wide leather band called a bandolier. Hanging from this are 12 leather containers – each holding a charge of powder – a leather bag filled with lead bullets, and a flask with spare powder. He also has a length of match, which is a cord boiled in vinegar. His gun is so heavy that it has to be balanced on a crutch of wood before firing. See if you can find out how a musket was fired.

Simon is not wearing any armour. He has on a buff jerkin, a doublet, breeches, thick hose and shoes.

How do you think it would feel to be fighting against your own father and brother? Why do you think men like Simon came to such a decision?

Try to find out more about soldiers' uniforms at the time of the Civil War.

A Disguise for Prince Charles, 1651

In 1649 Charles I was executed, and Oliver Cromwell, backed by the army, became the ruler of England. Young Prince Charles, however, was determined to reclaim the throne that his father had lost. He raised an army of loyal supporters but they were defeated by Cromwell at the battle of Worcester in 1651. Charles managed to escape from the battlefield and rode hard to Whiteladies on the Giffard family estate in Shropshire. Here he was taken in, fed and loaned the clothes of a working man, so that he would not be recognized when he tried to escape to France.

On the right you can see Charles being helped out of his own clothes by a manservant. He has already removed his lace collar, buff coat and hat with its jewelled hatband. Charles is wearing the most fashionable style of doublet, which is cut shorter than previously. It has slashed sleeves, through which his fine embroidered shirt can be seen. His matching breeches are open at the knee and trimmed with ribbons. Around the waist of the breeches are the hooks which are normally attached to the metal rings sewn inside the doublet to keep the suit together. He is also wearing fine leather boots and frilled boot hose.

The servant is not dressed as fashionably as his master, of course, but his clothes are still expensive, as he comes from a well-to-do family. He is wearing a lace collar, a doublet with slashed sleeves and turned-back cuffs, breeches which have been secured at the knee with ribbons, and leather shoes with shoe roses.

For his disguise, Charles was given a workman's coarse shirt, a green jerkin and a leather doublet. He also wore heavy black shoes and a sugarloaf hat. His friends cut his hair short and he rubbed soot from the chimney into his face and hands in order to make himself look workmanlike. How do you think it would feel for the King to wear coarse, rough clothes after being used to his own fine garments?

This was a dangerous and difficult time not only for Charles but also for those who risked their lives to help their King. You will meet some of them over the next few pages.

some of the clothing loaned to Prince Charles

A Miller, 1651

From Whiteladies Charles went a short distance to Boscobel House, where he was helped by the five Penderel brothers, who all lived on the Giffard estate. William was the tenant at Boscobel House, Humphrey was the miller at Whiteladies, John and George both worked on the estate and Richard, whom you met earlier, lived with their mother at a neighbouring farm.

Here is Humphrey the miller. He is wearing a cloth doublet with fitted sleeves, breeches which are secured just below the knee, woollen hose and leather shoes. He is carrying his felt hat. He is also wearing a white apron to protect his clothes from the flour.

Very often on large estates the miller, as an employee of the landowner, would be supplied with his clothing so that he would be wearing 'livery' like the other servants. It is possible, therefore, that Humphrey has not had to pay for his clothes.

Humphrey and his brothers were not very wealthy or well educated but they were loyal and devoted Royalists. Richard accompanied Charles on his first attempt to get to Wales, and William sheltered the King and gave him food. Later, all five brothers escorted Charles on the next stage of the journey, to Mosely Hall, with Charles mounted on Humphrey's cart horse.

See if you can find out more about this adventure, in particular the day that the King spent hidden in an oak tree at Boscobel House.

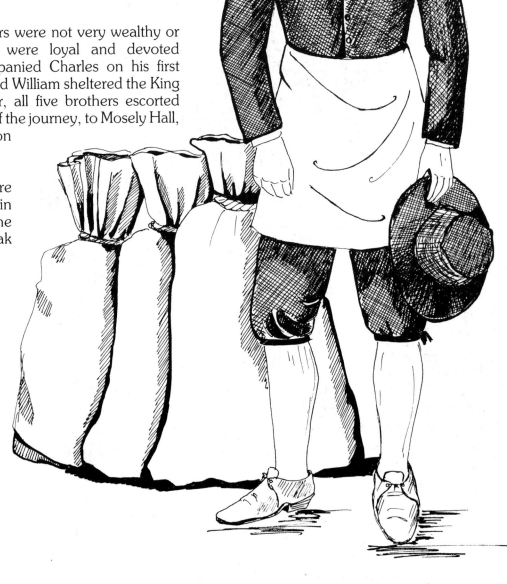

A Blacksmith, 1651

When Charles reached Mosely Hall he was made welcome by the owner, Thomas Whitgreave, who took him to a secret hiding place in the house, where he would be safe. While Charles was in hiding a group of Roundhead soldiers arrived looking for him. One of the soldiers wandered around to the back of the house away from the others and came across a smith shoeing a horse. The soldier tried to get information from the smith but he just carried on with his work and refused to say anything, even though there was a reward of £1000 on the King's head.

The smith is wearing a soft cap, a rough linen shirt, breeches, woollen hose and a leather apron with tassels. His shoes are called startups. These were often worn by country people and were loose fitting, made of leather and laced or buckled on the outer side. Later, the word 'startup' became corrupted to 'upstart' and was used to describe a person who had risen above his station in life.

A Fashionable Lady, 1651

This is Jane Lane, the sister of Colonel Lane of Bentley Hall, a country house four miles from Mosely.

She is wearing a wide linen collar with a lace border over her low-necked gown. The bodice of the gown is quite stiffly corsetted and laced at the back, and the skirt has been bunched up, revealing the embroidered underskirt beneath. Hairstyles have altered very little, except that the side curls are now longer, reaching to the shoulders. Aprons have become very popular, and Jane often wears a white embroidered one indoors.

When Jane goes out riding or on a journey, she often wears a safeguard – an overskirt which protects the skirt of her gown against dirt and helps keep her warm.

Jane undertook a dangerous journey with Charles. They set off for Bristol in the hope that Charles could find a ship there to take him to France. They went on horseback, with Charles riding pillion (riding on a light saddle in front of Jane). On the journey, the King disguised as Jane's manservant, wore a suit of country grey cloth like the Sunday best of a farmer's son. Despite his disguise the King found it hard to hide his refined manners, so the journey was often dangerous and they were in constant fear that he would be recognized.

It was several weeks before Charles finally reached France. In that time many people, from all walks of life, fed and sheltered him. He never forgot their kindness and rewarded many of them after the Restoration. See if you can find out more about some of these people and the costumes that they wore. Draw a picture of them and compare their clothing and lifestyles.

Fashionable couple, c. 1608

Charles I, c. 1638

A fashionable lady, c. 1642

Two serving maids, c. 1650

Commonwealth fashion, c. 1650

Fashion for 1670

Rich and poor, c. 1672

Female fashion, c. 1693

Male fashion, c. 1705

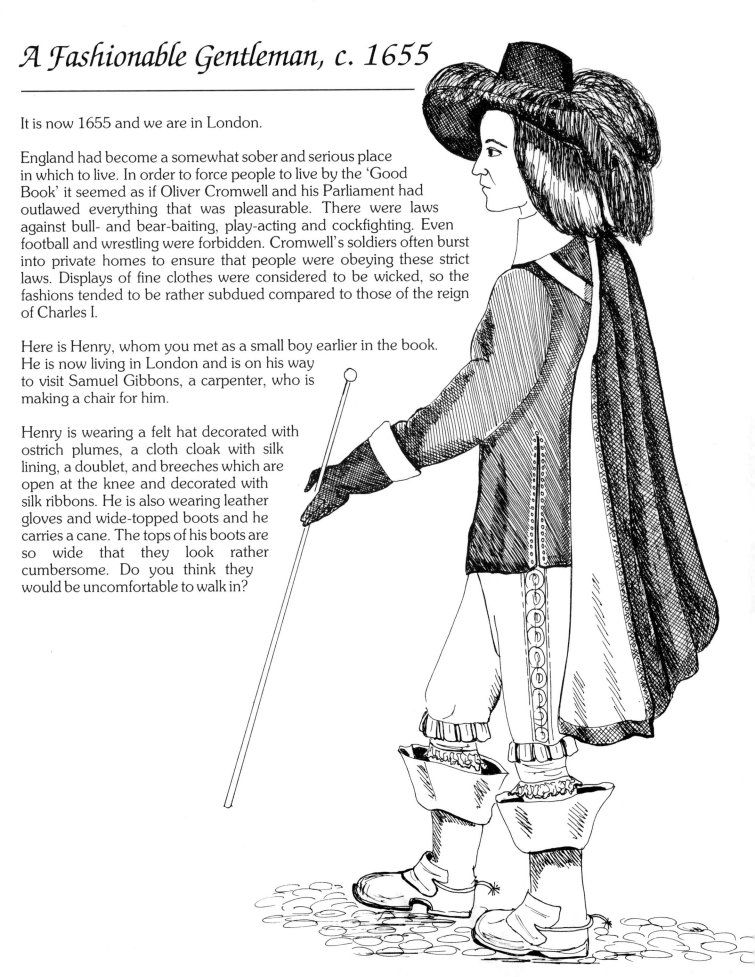

A Fashionable Gentleman, c. 1655

It is now 1655 and we are in London.

England had become a somewhat sober and serious place in which to live. In order to force people to live by the 'Good Book' it seemed as if Oliver Cromwell and his Parliament had outlawed everything that was pleasurable. There were laws against bull- and bear-baiting, play-acting and cockfighting. Even football and wrestling were forbidden. Cromwell's soldiers often burst into private homes to ensure that people were obeying these strict laws. Displays of fine clothes were considered to be wicked, so the fashions tended to be rather subdued compared to those of the reign of Charles I.

Here is Henry, whom you met as a small boy earlier in the book. He is now living in London and is on his way to visit Samuel Gibbons, a carpenter, who is making a chair for him.

Henry is wearing a felt hat decorated with ostrich plumes, a cloth cloak with silk lining, a doublet, and breeches which are open at the knee and decorated with silk ribbons. He is also wearing leather gloves and wide-topped boots and he carries a cane. The tops of his boots are so wide that they look rather cumbersome. Do you think they would be uncomfortable to walk in?

A Quaker Family, c. 1655

Here is Samuel Gibbons and his family. They are Quakers, which means that they belong to a religious sect which was founded by George Fox in 1650. Quakers thought very deeply about religion and were sober and serious people. They believed that everyone was equal and that there should be no ranks or classes in society. They read the Bible avidly and led lives that were bound by strict moral laws, with little time for relaxation or leisure. They dressed in plain clothes and drab colours and disapproved of ostentatious fashion and fine ornaments.

Samuel's wife, Rebecca, is wearing a brown linen dress which has been bunched up to reveal her plain underskirt beneath. She also has on a white linen cap and a deep collar. Her daughter, Patience, who is four years old, is wearing a white linen hood and collar, and a brown woollen dress with white cuffs and leading strings. Leading strings were often part of a child's dress in the seventeenth century and were used like the reins we have for little children today.

Baby Isaac is wearing a coif, a linen collar and apron and a plain wool dress. He is holding a rattle, which has bells attached and is tipped with coral.

Patience's doll is made of wood and is dressed as a smaller version of her mother. It is interesting that all the costumes on this page, including the doll's, are quite plain, with none of the frills and embroidery that we saw on the clothes of families earlier in the book.

The little stool below was made by Samuel, who is busy in his workshop.

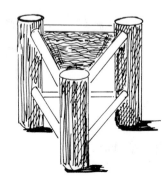

Samuel is wearing a white collar, a leather jerkin, old-fashioned breeches, woollen hose and stout leather shoes. His hair is very short. His sugarloaf hat and cloth cloak are hanging on the wall.

He is working on the chair that has been ordered by Henry. It is made of walnut, which is a softer wood than oak and therefore easier to carve. Samuel is a very skilled workman and takes a great pride in his work.

A relative of Samuel's, Grinling Gibbons (1648-1720), was another master craftsman in wood. In the inset picture below you can see an example of his work. It is a carving in limewood of a man's cravat, made to resemble linen and lace. It is a very fine and intricate piece of work. Perhaps you could find out more about the life of Grinling Gibbons and his beautiful carvings.

Also, try and discover more about the Puritans. In particular, the Pilgrims who left England to begin a new life in America in 1620. What kind of clothes would they have been wearing at that time?

A Nobleman at Court, c. 1663

In 1660, Charles II was restored to the throne, ending the oppressive rule of Oliver Cromwell and his son. Clothes suddenly became very extravagant, almost as if the new freedom had gone to people's heads. Everyone loved the French fashions that Charles brought with him from his exile, and they immediately became popular.

Here is Henry, who is now an adviser to the King. He is wearing a falling ruff in the form of a bib, a short doublet with paned sleeves, and petticoat breeches. These breeches resemble a divided skirt and are decorated with satin ribbons at the waist and sides. Henry also has ribbons on his doublet sleeves, shirt cuffs and shoes. He is carrying his plumed hat and a cane. He has shaved his head and is wearing a wig, as this is now more fashionable than long hair.

These fashions seem very fussy and extravagant to us, particularly the breeches which must have been very awkward at times. Samuel Pepys remarked to a friend in 1661 that he had put both legs through one leg hole of his petticoat breeches and 'went so all day'. How uncomfortable that must have been!

Petticoat breeches were sometimes worn with 'cannons'. These were decorative frills at the top of the stockings which were folded over garters to form flounces at the knee.

The soles of shoes were often slotted for hiding love letters or notes of political intrigue. Perfumed sachets were frequently carried in the wide-topped boots, and most men wore embroidered garters and gloves and carried handkerchiefs. Compare this extravagant and flamboyant style of dress with that of the Puritans and also with the fashions of today. Do you think men might wear these kind of clothes ever again?

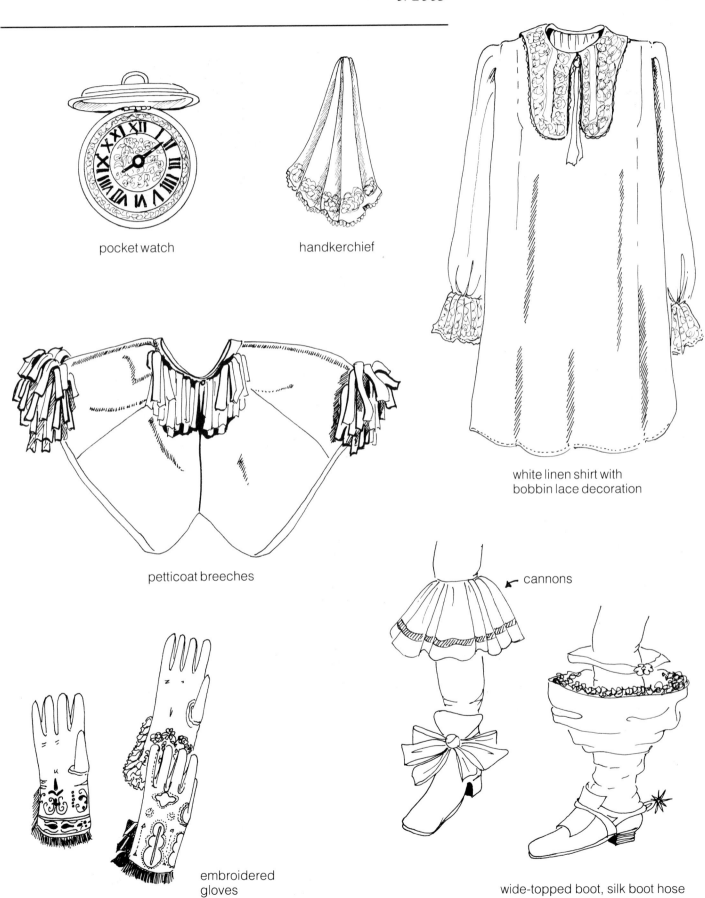

pocket watch

handkerchief

white linen shirt with
bobbin lace decoration

petticoat breeches

← cannons

embroidered
gloves

wide-topped boot, silk boot hose

The Nobleman's Wife, c. 1663

Here is Henry's wife, Catherine. She is dressed in the latest fashions. She is wearing a stiffened bodice with a low neckline which is decorated with a gauzy scarf. The bodice is very tight fitting and comes to a low point at the front. Her skirt is fastened up at the back to show the rich silk lining and her embroidered satin underskirt. She is also wearing matching pearl earrings, bracelets and necklace and she carries a perfumed fan.

Ladies' hairstyles have not altered very much, except that the side curls are now even longer. Sometimes, fancy curls were given special names – for example, 'confidants' were the smaller curls near the ears and 'creve-coeur' ('heartbreakers') were the two small curls at the nape of the neck. When Catherine goes out she often wears a limp hood rather than a hat so as not to spoil her ringlets.

On the opposite page you can see another of her gowns, which has different fastenings. The bodice is laced very tightly down the back and the skirt is secured up at the back with ribbons. Do you think it would be healthy to be so tightly corseted into a dress?

Catherine often wears patches on her face and she uses powder and rouge. Masks are still very popular for the theatre or out of doors for disguise. Catherine might wear a half mask, like that pictured opposite, or one which covers her whole face.

Have a look at some of her other accessories. In particular, the purse. Draw a purse like this to scale and design an embroidered pattern for it. How long do you think it would have taken to make such a purse by hand?

limp hood

silver scent bottle

canvas purse lined with silk and embroidered with metal thread – 12cm square

coney fur muff

muff bracelets for protecting the wrists

mask

leather shoe with applied silk braid

mule

patten

A Doctor, 1665

This is William, the farmer's son whom you met earlier. William studied hard and went to university so that he could become a doctor. He now has a thriving practice in London, where he lives with his wife and two young children.

William is reasonably well off, so he can afford the fashions of the day. He is wearing a boater-style hat decorated with ribbons, a curled wig and a muslin cravat with a lace edge. Over his doublet and petticoat breeches he is wearing a cassock. This is a loose, thigh-length coat, which widens towards the hem. It has a flat collar, turned-back cuffs and a back vent.

This is a sad and difficult time for William, as London is in the middle of a terrible plague epidemic. Thousands of people have died and many have fled from the city to escape infection. William has sent his own wife and children away but has remained in London himself to try to help the sick.

Little was known about the causes of the plague or how to treat it. Many doctors tried to protect themselves from infection by wearing tent-like garments of leather which reached to the ground. Over this they wore gauntlet gloves and hoods that completely covered their faces. The hoods had eye pieces made of glass and a beak which was filled with herbs to counteract the germs. This outfit must have been hot for the doctor and terrifying for his patients!

a doctor's plague hood

A Watchman, 1665

William has just been to Samuel Gibbons' house. Samuel's wife has been stricken with the plague, and because of this the whole family are in quarantine to avoid spreading the disease. (The word 'quarantine' comes from the Italian for 40, 'quaranta', and people were isolated, by law, for 40 days.) The door of their house has been locked and sealed and a red cross painted on it with the words 'Lord Have Mercy Upon Us'. A watchman, Thomas, is guarding the door so that no one can go in or out except for the doctor and the parson. Samuel has to give Thomas money to buy food and drink for his family. To do this, he passes a basket from an upper window to pay him and take in the goods. This means that the watchman avoids contact with the disease.

Thomas's clothes are practical rather than fashionable. He is wearing sugarloaf hat, a leather jerkin over a doublet, woollen breeches, stout leather shoes and leather gloves. He carries a red stave to warn people to keep away.

One of the reasons why the plague spread so rapidly was poor hygiene. Although many people looked very handsome in Stuart times, they rarely washed and often wore the same clothes for long periods at a time. In addition to this, the streets of London were full of garbage, human and animal excrement and were infested with rats, so it is not surprising that germs spread. Just stop to think about the contrast between the beauty and splendour of some of the clothes you have seen and the insanitary living conditions.

41

A Family in the Great Fire, 1666

Only a few months after the plague epidemic another disaster struck London. This was the Great Fire of 1666. It lasted for four days and destroyed thousands of houses and over 80 churches. Although the loss of life was not great, the fire left many people homeless, and thousands had to camp out in fields outside the city.

There was no fire brigade at this time. Instead leather buckets were provided by each parish and kept in the church ready for use in the event of fire. There were also huge syringes which were used to squirt water on the fire. It took three men to work one syringe: two men held the syringe, whilst a third worked the plunger, squirting a jet of water on the flames.

Here you can see Thomas, who, along with several other men, has been trying to quench the flames. He is wearing a leather fireman's helmet but apart from this he has no protective clothing.

Thomas's own house has been destroyed and his wife, Frances, and their children are begging him to go with them across the river to safety. Thomas wants to stay to try to fight the fire, but Frances is frightened that they will never find each other again if they become separated, for the streets are choked with terrified men, women and children all trying to escape.

Frances is wearing a white linen hood, a matching bodice and skirt and an apron which is tucked up into her belt. She has baby Hal strapped to her back. He is wearing a white hood and a woollen dress.

Agnès and Ben are twins. They are seven years old and are frightened and bewildered by everything. Agnès is wearing a woollen cap over her hood, a print shawl, an unmatching bodice and skirt and an apron. Ben has on a doublet and breeches, but he has no hat or shoes. Both children are carrying bundles of clothing.

After the devastation caused by the fire, people wanted to be sure they would be prepared in case of a similar event in the future. Gradually, fire insurance companies were formed. People paid small amounts of money to them to insure their homes, and they could then claim damages in the event of a fire. The insurance companies formed their own fire brigades, but they would only visit people who were insured with them. So insured people displayed a plaque on their house so that the fire brigades knew whom to help! These plaques had to be positioned quite high up so that they could not be stolen.

An Actress, c. 1667

During the Puritanical rule of Oliver Cromwell many theatres had been shut down as play going was considered wicked. Theatres enjoyed a revival under Charles II, however, who not only re-established those that had been closed, but also opened two new ones. Theatre-going suddenly became very fashionable and actors and actresses found a greater security in their work than they had had before.

One important change was that for the first time women appeared on stage to take the female parts. Previously these had been played by men or young boys. One of the most famous of these actresses was Nell Gwynne, who later became the King's mistress. Henry and Catherine would probably have seen her on one of their many visits to the theatre.

Nell joined the theatre as an orange girl when she was only 13. She would stand in the pit at the front of the auditorium with other girls and sell oranges to the audience – rather like our ice-cream and chocolate-sellers today.

Nell liked to wear loose, flowing clothes, so her garments do not appear quite as stiff as the other fashionable clothes that you have seen. Here she is wearing a chemise under a dress which has a fitted bodice and a loose, flowing skirt. She wears a muslin shawl around her shoulders and has her hair in long curls casually draped over her shoulder.

Nell soon became a leading actress and was loved by all who saw her. Samuel Pepys, after meeting her in her dressing room, could not forget her and called her 'pretty, witty Nell'. She was noted for her comic roles and John Dryden, a famous contemporary playwright, wrote parts especially for her.

On the far right, you can see her in her dressing room before a performance of *The Mayden Queen* by Dryden.

Nell has tied up her hair so that it is out of the way while she applies her make-up, and she is sitting in her undergarments. Her chemise has a low neck with a V-front fastening and a drawstring. The sleeves are quite large. Her corset is without shoulder straps because she is going to wear a low-necked dress. The corset is laced at the back, with imitation lacing at the front. It is stiffened with whalebone splints. If her dress were heavily laced or boned she would have no need of a corset like this – in fact, it would be almost impossible to wear the two together! Nell has on several linen petticoats and her satin shoes are lying on the floor.

She is busily applying rouge to her lips and cheeks. Can you identify some of the other objects on the bench?

Nell's undergarments are highly perfumed, for, like most women of that time, her personal hygiene leaves a lot to be desired!

Nell came from a notorious family. Her mother was an alcoholic and her sister Rose was at one time imprisoned for theft. Rose was married to a highwayman, whom you will meet on the next page.

45

A Highwayman, c. 1667

Getting from one place to another was a difficult and dangerous business in Stuart times. Roads were often impassable in bad weather, and highwaymen and bandits were a constant threat to travellers.

Here is Nell Gwynn's highwayman brother-in-law. Although he is reasonably well off after his exploits, he is not dressed in the latest fashions, as they would be impractical on horseback.

He is wearing a leather jerkin over his doublet, breeches, a low-crowned hat trimmed with a feather, a lace collar, a woollen cloak and fringed leather gloves. His boots are made of stiff, hard leather and have bucket tops which come up over the knee. They are pulled on without fastenings. Sometimes, he might wear a lighter pair of boots with high heels, like those in the picture below. Around his chest he wears a sword belt and he is carrying a flintlock pistol. You can see the pistol holder just under his left hand.

The penalties for highway robbery were severe. Usually the culprits were hanged and their dead bodies were hung by the roadside in a set of iron chains as a deterrent to other would-be offenders.

There were still many highwaymen, however, some of whom became quite famous. See if you can find out more about Claude Duval, the dashing Frenchman who came to England at the time of the Restoration. Another interesting character was Moll Cutpurse (whose real name was Mary Frith). Moll was one of the few successful highwaywomen. When you have found out more about them try drawing them in the costumes that they might have worn.

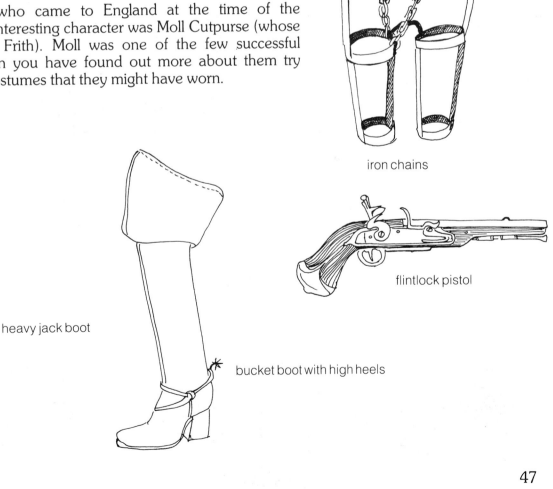

iron chains

flintlock pistol

heavy jack boot

bucket boot with high heels

A Lady of Fashion, c. 1680

We are now going to move forward to the year 1680. This is Eleanor, Henry and Catherine's eldest daughter. She has married a wealthy landowner who lives near Bath and they have two small children.

Eleanor can afford the latest, most fashionable, clothes, and here she is dressed for the winter. For warmth she is wearing a loose hood, tied under her chin, and a matching fur stole and muff. Under the stole she has on a tippet, which is a waist-length cape. It is now the fashion for the bodices and skirts of gowns to be joined and for them to have long trains. The skirt of Eleanor's gown is secured at the back with ribbons, revealing the beautiful lining and her petticoat, which has three lace flounces.

On the opposite page you can see another of her gowns, this time from the rear view. Once again, the skirt is bunched up at the back to show the lining and petticoats. All the frills, lace and ribbon on these gowns would be very costly. It is sad to think that the trains of dresses like these would trail in the mud and filth of the city streets!

Also pictured is Eleanor's fashionable new hairstyle, which is flatter on top than previously, with more width at the sides and long curls at the back.

Face patches are still very popular and sometimes Eleanor uses 'plumpers'. These are light, round balls made of cork which she uses to fill up the cavities of her cheeks! It would probably be quite difficult to talk with these in. What do you think?

You can also see some of her beautiful shoes and one of her purses. Her wardrobe contains several pairs of knitted silk stockings in the bright colours that are fashionable. Other accessories include many pairs of embroidered gloves, both wrist length and elbow length, and several pairs of lace and silk mittens for wearing in the summer.

the new hairstyle

lace cap with ribbons

shoe and clog

drawstring purse in silk, embroidered with silver thread

silk boudoir slipper with lace ruff

embroidered brocade shoe

rear view of gown

silk shoe

A Gentleman of Fashion, c. 1680

Here is Eleanor's husband, Oliver. You can see from his outfit that great changes have taken place in men's fashions. The doublet is no longer fashionable and, instead, men are wearing waistcoats and coats. The waistcoat was a long-sleeved garment at this time but was the forerunner of the waistcoat as we know it today.

Oliver is wearing a lace cravat with a wide bow at his neck, a long, lined cape with a collar, and he carries a muff for warmth. His coat is quite loose and has low pockets. As he is wearing it unbuttoned his waistcoat is visible beneath. His breeches are less bulky than previously and are secured at the knee. His leather gloves are decorated with a thick fringe and his hat with an ostrich feather. On the opposite page there is a picture of one of his suits. From this you can see the shape of the coat more clearly.

Sometimes, when it is cold, Oliver wears his overcoat. This is called a 'brandenburg', after the Prussian city famous for its wools.

Boots are no longer fashionable for street wear and are generally only worn for riding, so Oliver has a large collection of shoes.

Wigs were still very popular. Small rollers of pipe clay called 'bilboquets', or 'roulettes', were used to tighten the curls. The roulettes were heated first. Hair powders and dyes were used on both wigs and natural hair, and combing one's wig in public was a very fashionable thing to do! How hygienic do you think it would be to wear a wig all the time?

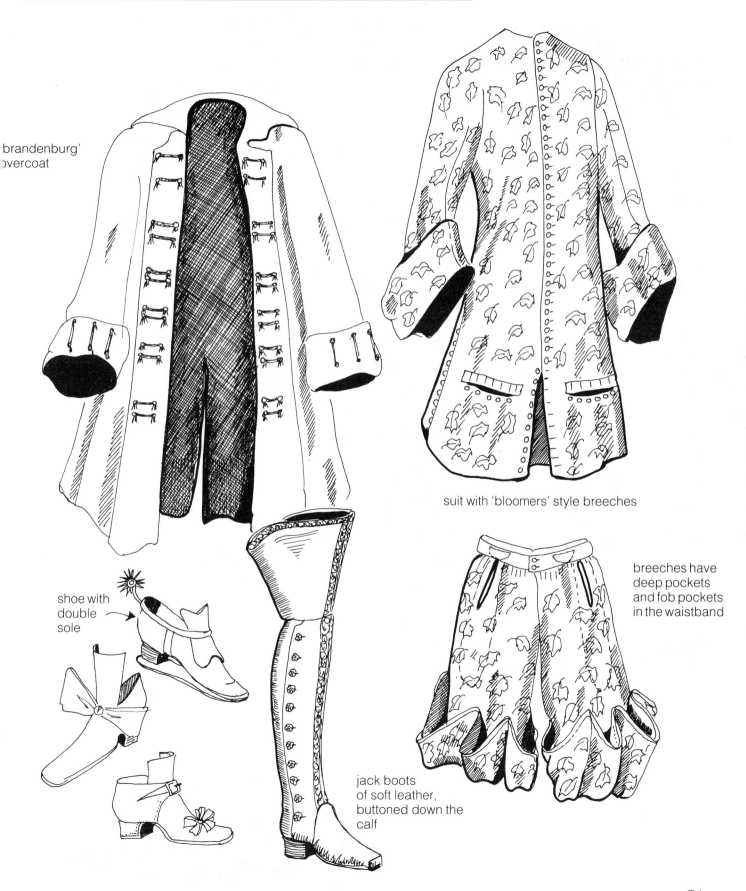

'brandenburg' overcoat

suit with 'bloomers' style breeches

shoe with double sole

breeches have deep pockets and fob pockets in the waistband

jack boots of soft leather, buttoned down the calf

A Coffee Shop, c. 1685

At this time it was the fashion for wealthy gentlemen to visit the new coffee houses that were springing up around the country. Here they would enjoy good coffee, intellectual conversation and read the newspapers that were kept for the customers.

Oliver likes to go to Sally Lunn's coffee house in Bath. Sally came to England from France in 1680 as a Huguenot refugee. She quickly became famous for her delicious buns, which were rather like the French *brioche*, and soon everyone was asking for a 'Sally Lunn bun'. Here you can see Oliver at her shop. He is wearing a long coat and patterned waistcoat. His cravat has lace edging and his shirt has frilled cuffs.

Sally is wearing a plain woollen dress with the sleeves rolled back and the skirt tucked up into her belt, displaying the lining. She has a partlet fill-in at her neck and a white cotton hood and apron.

Walter is the kitchen boy at Sally's shop. He does all sorts of odd jobs like fetching, carrying, washing and cleaning. It is hard work and he gets very tired, but on the whole he is happy, for Sally is a kind mistress.

Walter's outfit is very simple, consisting of a shirt, woollen breeches, hose, shoes and a white apron. It would be impractical for him to wear smart, fine clothes for his job and, besides, Walter's parents cannot afford them.

See if you can find out more about coffee houses in the seventeenth century. In particular, the origins of the London Stock Exchange.

Two Street-Vendors, c. 1685

City streets were lively and noisy places in Stuart times, as pedlars, hawkers and street-sellers wandered up and down calling out and parading their wares.

Walter's parents are both street-vendors. Arthur, his father, bakes his own pastries (though Walter thinks that they are not as nice as Sally Lunn's!) and sells them in the streets to passers-by.

Arthur is wearing an overcoat, which is fastened at the back, a shirt, breeches and a white apron. His hat has a flat crown because he has to balance his basket on his head. His shoes do not have fashionable high heels as this would be impractical for someone who spends all day on his feet.

Arthur has many friends who are street-sellers. Among them are a water-seller, a milk-seller and a song-seller. Can you find out what they would be wearing?

c. 1685

Arthur's wife, Clarice, is in another street. She is selling oranges. She is wearing a flat-crowned hat over a limp hood and has a plain woollen gown. The skirt of her gown is drawn together at the back so that it is her shorter underskirt that is exposed to the wear and tear of street walking. Clarice's feet are constantly wet and muddy, but pattens would be impractical because she has so many hours of walking and standing.

Arthur and Clarice are not wealthy. They have to make their clothes last for a long time, and Clarice repairs them when they become worn. In the winter, Clarice borrows one of Arthur's overcoats to keep her warm.

Street-selling is a precarious business. Arthur and Clarice are grateful to Sally Lunn for giving Walter a job in her kitchen, for the little extra money he earns is very useful. Their other son, 12-year-old Sam, also sells pastries in the streets.

The New Fashions, c. 1693

It is now 1693. Here is Eleanor, dressed in the latest fashions.

Her gown has an open bodice which is filled in with a stomacher. The sleeves are short and have buttoned-up cuffs, revealing the deep frill on the sleeves of her chemise. Her skirt is secured up at the back and has a train.

Under her skirt she is wearing a bustle. This is a small pad which helps to raise the skirt at the back. Her petticoat has a floral design and a reverse flounce. At her neck she is wearing a steinkirk, a long cravat which is popular with both men and women. It is loosely tied and twisted, and the ends are secured either with a brooch or by being placed through a buttonhole. This cravat was named after the battle of Steinkirk, which was fought between the English and French in 1692. When the French officers went into action they did so in such a hurry that they did not have time to tie their cravats properly – and so a new fashion began!

Eleanor's headdress is called a 'fontange'. It is made up of a small cap with several pieces of folded lace wired up at the front and has long ends hanging at the back which she usually wears draped over her shoulders. This fashion originated in France when Mademoiselle Fontanges, the King's mistress, tied her long hair up out of the way with a ribbon when out riding. From this the fashion for bows and frills on the top of the head developed.

On the far right you can see another of Eleanor's outfits from side view, which displays the fontange and bustle more clearly. It is fashionable to wear a small apron, and Eleanor has several in her wardrobe, some of which are beautifully embroidered.

c. 1693

Look carefully at the dress on the left below. It is not one of Eleanor's but a dress from the year 1874 – 182 years later! Compare the two styles; the bustle, the lace and ribbon trimmings and turned-back cuffs. Can you think of any other examples of fashion repeating itself like this?

(c.1874)

Eleanor's Children, c. 1693

Here are three of Eleanor's children. Anthony, the eldest, is 15, and he is soon going off to Oxford University, where he will study Latin and Greek. Not many other subjects were taught at universities at this time. Mathematics, for example, was considered to be suitable only for tradesmen. Anthony is interested in science, however, so his father will pay for a private tutor so that he can study it in his spare time.

Christopher is seven and little Barbara is five. You can see that it is still the custom to dress small children as miniature adults, and Anthony's and Christopher's outfits are very similar.

Their coats are quite wide, due to the pleats in either side which make them stand out from the waist. The pockets have flaps, and are not merely slits as they were previously, and they have buttoned-up cuffs.

Both boys are wearing cravats, although Anthony's is worn in the steinkirk fashion, and both have velvet breeches. Their hats have turned-up brims and are decorated with feathers. Their shoes have square toes, large square tongues, and buckles. Anthony is wearing rolled-up stockings and garters. Christopher's waistcoat is visible beneath his coat. It is made of silk and is beautifully patterned. Christopher does not wear a wig but has his own long hair brushed up high from the crown.

Barbara is wearing a fashionable fontange headdress without the side pieces. Her gown is very stiff and formal. The bodice comes to a point at the front and has a stomacher insert. The sleeves are short and have turned-back lace cuffs. The skirt has an open front with a lace underskirt and a train at the back. Barbara has leading strings hanging from the shoulders of her gown.

Look back at the clothes of Cecily, Henry and James, c. 1632 (pages 16 and 17). How have children's clothes changed since the beginning of the century? Who do you think looks the most comfortable?

Conclusion

Now we come to the end of the Stuart period. Fashions changed very little during the reign of Queen Anne. You can see an example of an early eighteenth-century costume in the colour section.

As we have seen, the Stuart period was a time of conflicts, disasters, romance and gaiety. All of these were reflected in the clothes that people wore, from the severity of Puritan dress to the romantic frills and finery that Charles II brought back from France at the time of the Restoration. We must remember, however, that fashions were worn only by the wealthy and that the clothes of poorer people changed very little over the century.

Fabrics were extremely expensive, especially imported silks, and because of this there was an important market in second-hand clothes and materials.

The couple pictured here are street-sellers like Arthur and Clarice. They deal in second-hand clothes.

Martha is wearing a conical-crowned wide-brimmed hat over a hood. Her gown is quite plain, having a fitted bodice with a stomacher insert, short sleeves and a floor-length skirt. She is wearing a plain white apron to protect her dress, and her frilled chemise sleeves are visible at her elbows.

In her basket she has pieces of second-hand materials, such as taffeta and velvet, which she hopes to sell to passers-by.

Unlike Eleanor and her family, who have their clothes made up by a tailor, Martha makes all her own clothes, as do many of her customers, who are only too pleased to be able to buy cheap materials from her.

Martha's husband, Walter, is in another street. He is selling second-hand clothes. He is wearing an old cape over a worn woollen coat, plain breeches and unmatching shoes. Around his neck he has a piece of old linen instead of a cravat. He does not wear a fashionable wig and has three wide-brimmed hats on his head all of which he hopes to sell. He is carrying other items of second-hand clothing.

Walter's outfit is made up from some of his unsold stock, so his clothing is a good example of costume relating to the wearer's occupation!

Bear this in mind as you reflect on the costumes in this book. How do clothes reflect people's lifestyles and occupations? Could you look around in the streets today and guess what people do for a living by looking at their clothes?

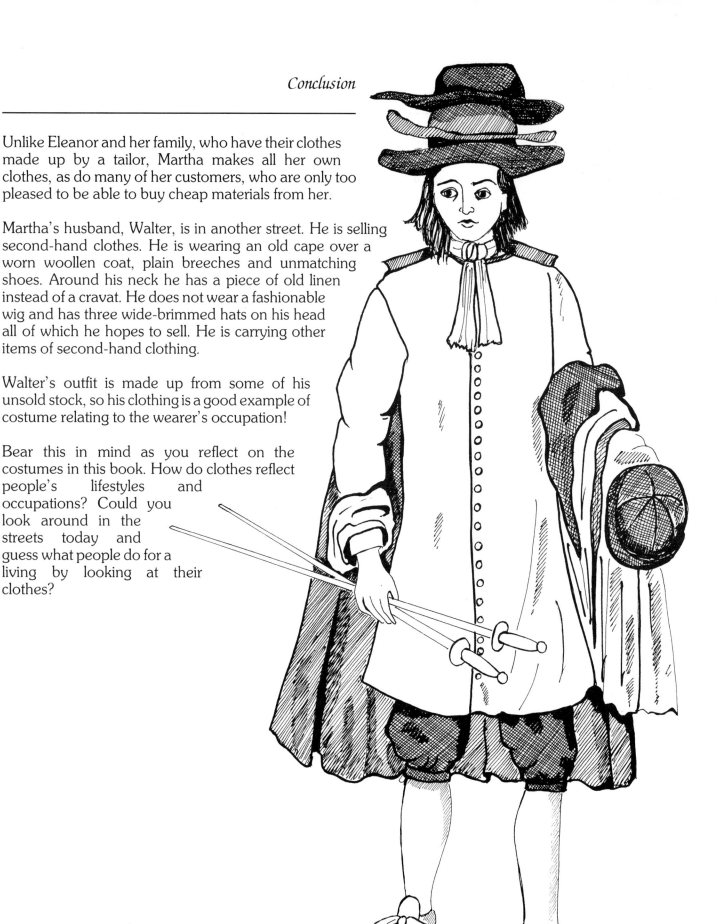

Glossary

aiglets	decorative metal tags on the ends of points (*page 8*)
bandolier	a shoulder belt used by soldiers for carrying ammunition (*pages 25 and 27*)
basque	a band of material attached to the bodice at the waistline (*pages 12 and 16*)
bilboquets (or roulettes)	small rolls of pipe clay used for curling wigs (*page 50*)
boot hose	coarse stockings worn over silk stockings for protection (*pages 12, 28 and 37*)
brandenburg	a thick, loose winter coat (*page 51*)
buff coat	of military origin, worn for protection (*pages 25 and 26*)
bustle	a pad of material worn under the skirt to make it stand out at the back (*pages 56 and 57*)
butterfly spur leathers	spur leathers with a distinctive butterfly shape (*pages 12, 20, 25 and 33*)
cannons	decorative frills on the top of stockings and worn with petticoat breeches (*page 37*)
cassock	a loose overcoat – the forerunner of the brandenburg (*page 40*)
cloak-bag breeches	full oval breeches gathered at the waist and shaped in above the knees (*page 19*)
coif	a close-fitting linen cap tied under the chin with strings (*pages 23 and 34*)
cornet	an embroidered linen cap (*page 10*)
doublet	a man's close-fitting jacket, worn over a shirt (*pages 8, 12, 19, 20, 29, 30, 33 and 36*)
earstring	a few strands of silk threaded through the ear and worn for decoration (*page 8*)
falling ruff	a cross between a lace collar and a stiff ruff (*pages 13, 18 and 19*)
farthingale	a wheel-shaped structure made of whalebone or wire and used to make ladies' skirts stand out (*pages 10 and 11*)
fontange	a lady's headdress consisting of a small cap worn on the back of the head with several pieces of folded lace wired up at the front (*pages 56, 57 and 59*)
French roll	a padded roll worn around the waist under the skirt to give fullness to the dress at the hips (*page 11*)
jack boots	men's boots of two styles: either made of stiff, hard leather with square bucket tops, or made of softer leather, laced or buttoned at the sides (*pages 47 and 51*)
jerkin	a man's close-fitting jacket made of leather, usually without sleeves. If sleeves were present they were made of material rather than leather (*pages 28, 35, 41 and 42*)
leading strings	streamers attached to small children's dresses at the shoulders and used rather like children's reins today (*pages 34 and 59*)
livery	clothing issued to servants by their master (*page 30*)
lobster tail helmet	a helmet worn by soldiers during the Civil War (*page 25*)
love-lock	a curled lock of hair grown long and brought forward from the nape of the neck to rest on the shoulder (*page 13*)
mastic	a gum, or resin, taken from the bark of certain trees (*page 15*)
muckinder	a handkerchief (*page 16*)
panes	bands of cloth joined together at the ends and used for decoration (*pages 14, 16 and 36*)
pantoffles	overshoes used to protect the footwear (*page 13*)
partlet	a separate fill-in for covering the neck and chest (*pages 14 and 52*)
pattens	wooden overshoes raised on iron rings (*pages 22 and 39*)
plumpers	light, round balls made of cork and used to fill out hollow cheeks (*page 48*)
petticoat breeches	men's wide breeches resembling a divided skirt (*pages 36, 37 and 40*)
points	laces used to fasten one garment to another (*pages 8 and 9*)
safeguard	an overskirt used when travelling for protection and warmth (*page 32*)
slashing	cutting slits of varying lengths into a garment for decoration (*pages 12, 18, 19, 24 and 29*)
startup	high, loose-fitting shoes of rough leather, laced on the outer side (*page 31*)
steinkirk	a long, lace-edged cravat, loosely tied and twisted, with the ends secured either with a brooch or by placing through a buttonhole; named after the battle of Steinkirk in 1692 (*pages 56 and 58*)
stomacher	an ornamental panel made of embroidered material and inserted into the front of a doublet or gown (*pages 56 and 60*)
sugarloaf hat	a hat with a high conical crown and broad brim (*pages 21, 28 and 35*)
swaddling	the custom of bandaging a tiny baby from head to toe in order to protect it and to enable it to grow straight (*page 17*)
tippet	a cape reaching to just below the waist (*page 48*)
underpropper	a wire frame used to support a lace collar (*pages 8 and 10*)

Book List

Asquith, Stuart A.	*The Campaign of Naseby, 1645*, Osprey Publishing, 1979
Black, J.A. & Garland, M.	*A History of Fashion*, Orbis Publishing, 1975
Bradfield, Nancy	*Historical Costumes of England 1066-1956*, Harrap, 1958
Brook, Iris	*English Costume of the Seventeenth Century*, Black, 2nd ed. 1950
Calthrop, Dion Clayton	*English Costume*, Black, 1941
Cassin-Scott, Jack	*Costume and Fashion 1550-1760*, Blandford Press, 1975
Contini, Mila	*Fashion from Ancient Egypt to the Present Day*, Hamlyn, 1965
Cumming, Valerie	*A Visual History of Costume: the Seventeenth Century*, Batsford, 1984
Cunningham, Peter	*Nell Gwynn*, Gibbings & Co, 1903
Cunnington, C.W. & P.	*Handbook of English Costume in the Seventeenth Century*, Faber, 1955
Cunnington, C.W. & P.	*History of Underclothes*, Faber, 1981
Cunnington, P.	*Costume of Household Servants from the Middle Ages to 1900*, Black, 1974
Cunnington, P. & Buck, A.	*Children's Costume in England 1300-1900*, Black, 1965
Cunnington, C.W. & Lucas, C.	*Occupational Costume in England*, Black, 1967
Falkus, Christopher	*The Life and Times of Charles II*, Weidenfeld and Nicolson, 1972
Foster, Vanda	*Costume Accessories: Bags and Purses*, Batsford, 1982
Jones, Madeline	*Growing Up in Stuart Times*, Batsford, 19XX
Latham, Robert (ed.)	*The Illustrated Pepys*, Bell and Hyman, 1978
Lister, Margot	*Costumes of Everyday Life*, Barrie and Jenkins, 1972
London Museum	*Men's Costume 1580-1750*, H.M.S.O., 1970
Masters, Brian	*The Mistresses of Charles II*, Blond and Briggs, 1979
Mendes, Linda	*Living Through History: The English Civil War*, Batsford, 1987
Millar, Oliver	*The Tudor, Stuart and Early Georgian Pictures in the Collection of Her Majesty the Queen*, Phaedon Press, 1968
Miller, Peggy	*Life in Stuart London*, Methuen, 1977
	Pictorial Encyclopaedia of Fashion, Hamlyn, 1968
Sichel, Marion	*Costume Reference, Volume 3: Jacobean, Stuart and Restoration*, Batsford, 1977
Trease, Geoffrey	*Samuel Pepys and His World*, Thames and Hudson, 1972
Truman, Nevil	*Historic Costuming*, Pitman, 1936
Watson, D.R.	*The Life and Times of Charles I*, Weidenfeld and Nicolson, 1979
Wilson, Eunice	*A History of Shoe Fashion*, Pitman, 1974

Places to Visit

Here are a few ideas for some interesting places to visit which should help you in your study of Stuart life and costume:

Bath Museum of Costume, Assembly Rooms, Bath, Avon.

Boscobel House, Near Shifnal, Shropshire.

Gallery of English Costume, Platt Hall, Platt Fields, Rusholme, Manchester M14 5LL.

Geffrye Museum, Kingsland Road, Shoreditch, London E2 8EA.

London Museum, Barbican, London.

The Verney Collection, Claydon House, Buckinghamshire.

The Victoria and Albert Museum, Cromwell Road, South Kensington, London SW7 2RL.

Things to Do

1. Try making a ruff or a fontange from material or paper. How do you think it would feel to have to wear one of these all day?

2. Find out more about the manufacture of textiles in the seventeenth century. Design some fabrics for yourself, using bright colours and intricate patterns. Make them suitable for a nobleman or his wife at the beginning of Stuart times.

3. Look at the various forms of make-up used by the Stuarts – both men and women. What were they made from? Draw some pictures of the different fashions in face patches, hairstyles and wigs.

4. Draw some coloured pictures of different soldiers' uniforms in the Civil War.

5. Find out all you can about some of these famous people from Stuart times:
   Daniel Defoe (1660-1731)
   Thomas Fairfax (1612-1671)
   Guy Fawkes (1570-1606)
   'Judge' Jeffreys (1645-89)
   Andrew Marvell (1621-1678)
   Samuel Pepys (1633-1703)
   Sir Christopher Wren (1632-1723)
   Draw pictures of them and try to get their costume as accurate as you can.

6. Think about life 'above and below the stairs' in Stuart times. Draw a picture of a wealthy family in their beautiful costumes and then draw another picture of some of the servants who work for them.

7. Find out more about various accessories that were popular in the seventeenth century – for example, fans, sticks, muffs, gloves, handkerchiefs and jewellery.

8. Bath became a very fashionable place in the seventeenth century. Find out more about leisure pursuits that were popular – for example, bathing in the spa waters. What kind of people might have used these facilities? What kind of clothes would they have been wearing?